PATIOS

FRANCES LINCOLN LIMITED
PUBLISHERS

PATIOS

ANDI CLEVELY

PHOTOGRAPHY BY
STEVEN WOOSTER

Frances Lincoln Ltd
4 Torriano Mews
Torriano Avenue
London NW5 2RZ
www.franceslincoln.com

First Frances Lincoln edition: 2007

A catalogue record for this book is available from the British Library.

ISBN 10: 0-7112-2642-3
ISBN 13: 978-0-7112-2642-5

Printed and bound in Singapore

9 8 7 6 5 4 3 2 1

A patio can provide opportunities for flower gardening (page 1), leisurely appreciation of the surrounding landscape (page 2), or simply sitting and relaxing in congenial company (this page).

CONTENTS

INTRODUCTION

The best of both worlds

The patio has become an established feature in modern gardens, largely thanks to the insight of the mid-twentieth-century American landscape architect Thomas Church. He drew on much earlier traditions from Persia and Moorish Spain, taking their typical courtyard gardening style and reinventing it for wealthy Californians to create an outdoor play space.

Inevitably the liberating trend towards open-plan arrangements indoors spread into the garden, taking in the area of ground next to the house as an extension of the living and dining rooms. As a concept this was a huge success and provided somewhere permanent and hospitable for celebrating life in the open air. It was a revolution, overturning received opinion about house and garden as separate territories and creating a valuable new garden space that fused the best of both worlds, indoors and out.

The essential elements of a perfect patio: attractive all-weather paving, a setting of lush refreshing foliage, comfortable seating and a table laid ready for indulgence.

Extreme possibilities: a humdrum courtyard and passageway (left) is transformed with decking and specimen container plants, while a grand covered terrace (right) flanking one side of a large house becomes an elegant and airy viewing gallery for the garden.

Definitions

Modern gardeners distinguish clearly between patios, courtyards and terraces, even though these frequently overlap in original meaning and many key features.

- Courtyard: a hard-surfaced space enclosed on all sides by buildings or walls and open to the sky, comprising often the entire garden although sometimes a work area close to the house.
- Patio: once meaning an inner courtyard, but now a separate hard-surfaced garden area, usually (but not necessarily) adjoining the house and often intended primarily for sitting or entertaining outdoors.
- Terrace: strictly speaking, a patio with a low surrounding wall or rail, although also used to describe a flat area formed from a slope when levelling ground for cultivation.

Patios are now so familiar and widespread that it is difficult to appreciate their early emancipating impact on gardening styles and activities as old boundaries and inhibitions disappeared, encouraging everyone to rediscover life alfresco. A patio can open the door to an outdoor living room, as full of promise and possibilities as a plot of soil for any keen gardener.

No space too small

The typical ancient Persian patio garden was a large domestic courtyard: basically a room without a ceiling that could offer shelter, refreshment and space for recreation in the midst of burning heat and barren, parched surroundings.

The modern counterpart is an equally special place, a green refuge in a built-up neighbourhood, or perhaps an island floor space within a busy, planted garden. Imaginatively conceived and developed, it can be an irresistible oasis for people and plants alike.

Its size is infinitely flexible. If you have the space or a yearning for grandeur, your patio could be an atrium

occupying the whole central area enclosed by walls or buildings; a terrace running the full width of the back of the house; or even a raised veranda or porch at the front where you can sit and watch the world go by – a rocking chair might be an essential accessory here.

At its other extreme a patio need be no more than a private corner of the garden, paved in some way and perhaps fitted out with somewhere to sit. Japanese gardening traditions consider a tiny courtyard just 1.2m (4ft) square adequate for contemplation (see box), and simple patio arrangements of this kind could easily be made on a balcony or rooftop, or in a city-centre basement area.

Letting in ideas

History and tradition can offer examples for inspiration and suggest ways to make your patio design more interesting or help you overcome apparent difficulties. There are very few rules that you have to follow.

You can adjust size, shape and alignment to suit the site and your requirements. The range of building materials is not limited to paving slabs or timber decking, and can include more inspired materials like metal grilles and glass gravel, whimsical patterns in mosaic, or a juxtaposition of several styles. Any material is worth considering; it is how you use it that determines success.

Furnishing the finished patio with water and lighting features, seats in bright colours or exotic plants in bold containers can all help you stamp your taste and personality on the simplest plan, turning it from a plain practical structure into an inviting outdoor room.

Although the design can be almost anything you want it to be, important decisions need to be made before starting the work, even if all you are doing is attempting to improve an existing inadequate feature. A patio is as permanent as any other building structure in the garden, and to make sure the finished project matches your vision, it is best to:

- Clarify exactly what you want from it.
- Assess what is there in terms of site and surroundings.
- Consider all the practical options on offer.

The result could be a highly prized and hard-working feature that will transform outdoor living for you.

The tsubo-niwa

This is a classic Japanese courtyard, intended for meditation and based in size on an old unit of area, the tsubo (equal to 1.4 sq.m or 36 sq.ft). Typically restrained and uncluttered, it might contain little more than a bowl of water, a dwarf maple and one or two rocks, lovingly chosen and sensitively placed to represent the elements of an ideal landscape.

This symphony of surfacing materials – timber, gravel, natural stone and moss – satisfies all the essential natural ingredients of an authentic oriental-style patio.

1

A GARDEN to LIVE IN

Simple in outline but infinitely variable in detail, a patio or courtyard is a classic garden feature that can become a cherished and lasting asset, the focus for a host of outdoor activities from alfresco entertaining to displaying a special collection of treasured plants. To make the most of the opportunities it offers, you need to balance aspiration with an appreciation of its special qualities so that it becomes a satisfying expression of your lifestyle and personal interests.

A PATIO PROFILE

Whereas most other components of a traditional garden are intended mainly as habitats for growing or displaying plants, patios and courtyards are primarily intermediate areas that blur the simple distinction between house and outdoors. Appreciating this merging of identities can be a liberating influence if you are used to the garden as a view from the window or somewhere synonymous with work, and it is part of the distinctive patio appeal.

A patio is as much part of the built environment as a component of the garden itself. Rather than lawn or bare soil, the base is a hard floor of timber or inorganic material such as stone or brick that provides a low-maintenance, all-weather surface. With their good drainage and drying capabilities, these surfaces are ideal places to arrange and keep all the accessories of outdoor living, adding the atmosphere of a sophisticated play space, perhaps, or a bistro. Weatherproof seating can be left in place as an invitation to slip out at the first hint of good weather, while barbecues and dining furniture look more in keeping here than in the open garden. A patio is somewhere to combine the art of interior decoration with relaxation and gardening, often in the style of Mediterranean life outdoors.

Many plants revel in the patio environment. Depending on its aspect (the amount of light, warmth and shelter the

Wood is a versatile paving material which can be stained and finished to suit a tasteful, almost ceremonial scheme (previous pages) or left natural as an unsophisticated base for a cheerfully informal back garden patio (left).

Climate Change

In full sun patio floors reflect some of the day's warmth into the immediate surroundings and absorb the rest like a storage heater, retaining it by day and then releasing it into the evening air. When this capability is combined with the similar storage properties of a courtyard's walls, there is a heat increment that can add an average of 2–3°C (3–5°F) to the area, or as much as 6°C (10°F) on a bright sunny day.

While extra heat is often desirable in a cool climate, in hotter regions, where escape from the sun may be a high priority, a shaded patio positioned near water or in the path of cooling breezes can offer welcome relief. Supplementing the effect of shaded surfaces with water features and plenty of leafy plants can tangibly cool the area and make it feel more congenial.

patio receives), you can grow specialized subjects such as shade-lovers, succulents that bask in sun and heat, trained fruit in ornamental containers, a collection of bonsai trees arranged on airy shelves or a riotous display of seasonal bedding in raised beds. Lack of soil is no constraint, while growing in containers that can be moved round the patio according to the season is an advantage, allowing greater flexibility than permanent planting in the garden.

The patio as a stage

Although it offers a host of unique planting opportunities (see Chapter 3), the modern patio is above all a practical living space planned for people, a stage that can be dressed and managed for special occasions as well as everyday purposes.

Even if it is tucked away in a secret corner of the garden, there is a psychological spotlight on the patio as somewhere out of the ordinary where you can retreat, gather or make merry. You need to set the scene well, but not so thoroughly that there is no scope for your tastes and activities to change and evolve. As it is also a permanent major feature – in the case of a courtyard, often the entire garden – while dreaming and scheming you should be confident that the maturing design will match its location as well as your lifestyle, while at the same time remaining adaptable.

The classically austere outlines of carefully groomed hedges and topiary complement the immaculate pavement of tightly packed bricks.

PREPARING TO PLAN

Getting the design right depends on careful early planning, starting ideally with a look at your own motives and aspirations. The most obvious question you need to answer first is why?, before exploring where? and how?. Your answers will give you pointers towards using the space to best effect. If you want to extend the living room, leaving sliding doors open so that you can move easily in and out of the sun, the patio will need to abut the house like a terrace, as a place where children at play can be safe or supervised, and it is not far to run from the rain. If you entertain regularly, you might need to allow space for seating large numbers of guests.

Think about how many people might use the patio at one time, whether they will tend to be family or formal visitors, and when you are most likely to use it: a bright open aspect is more appropriate for sunbathing, whereas summer evening entertaining could benefit from a position where you can watch the sun go down. Your emphasis might be primarily on a patio as an outdoor room, with

Piercing a patio screen with a window or doorway reveals a seductive glimpse of welcome relaxation and, in this example, allows refreshing breezes laden with the scent of flowering lavender.

floor space, furniture and accessories such as heat and light, or as a garden area in which to grow a special range of plants. If the latter, be honest about how much you enjoy gardening, and whether you might appreciate a low-maintenance emphasis.

Once the main purpose is established, elaborate the picture with some basic details.

If you entertain, for example, will you cook outside on a barbecue, chiminea or fire pit (in which case the patio could be sited far from the house), or do you need to be near the kitchen, with easy access to and fro? Visualize the perfect atmosphere: cool and sophisticated with seclusion and subtle lighting, or perhaps a street-café style with plenty of plants, bright colours and lively cadences from playing water.

If your aim is an oasis of green peace, decide if this needs to be near the house so that you can enjoy the plants from indoors, or at the bottom of the garden, perhaps where you can sit under trees with your back to the world. Would you prefer the calm formality of a few majestic plants in choice containers and symmetrical beds, a lush jungle of exotic and tropical foliage, or an escape into a disorderly wilderness of wild flowers, bird feeders and a natural pond?

Comfort and safety can be important for family or guests alike, and these may affect the design. Raised patios may need handrails (check local Building Regulations about these) and steps might be used by children and elderly or disabled people. If there is to be a play space for children, remember that moving water is less dangerous than a still pool, however shallow; a sandpit can benefit from a lid to exclude pets; and installations such as swings need secure anchorage (often easier on a timber deck than a paved floor) and soft landing areas. Storage places could be built in to keep play materials and fold-up furniture safe and dry.

Matching reality

It is good to dream and explore sources of inspiration, but equally important is a review of the site: what you would like and what you have got may be poles apart. No space is beyond improvement, however, and apparent liabilities can be turned into assets or opportunities for adapting and improving the original plans.

At this stage you need to be detached and practical. Feelings of alarm at a neglected site or impatience to get started on a new one can jeopardize the best of plans, and honest appraisal early on can help avoid unnecessary cost, frustration or disappointment later.

Multi-purpose props

Where space is rationed, adapt furniture and fittings for changing use:

- Chairs and benches double as storage boxes for tools or folding stools.
- A tabletop can open to reveal a barbecue.
- Cap walls of raised beds with comfortable slabs for seats.
- Cut holes in a tabletop to hold pots of growing tomatoes and salad leaves.
- Position tiles among a herb planter to rest plates and pick your own garnish.
- Sink a children's sandpit where it is easy to cover and change later to a pond.

The new garden Recently built housing and grassed-down or cleared gardens are clean slates on which to overlay a basic design. You will need to keep an eye on balance in the garden and the impact a patio might make on the remaining space and any further plans. But compared with other situations you have carte blanche to design what you like – even to turn the whole garden into a paved area or build more than one patio.

The established garden More circumspection is needed here. A patio could supply the missing link between

Paving works both as a neutral or passive background and as a key design ingredient, as here, where the same mellow bricks are used deliberately to unite the octagonal island patio with the herringbone-patterned path.

house and garden, but equally might obliterate favourite areas and compete with the rest if you are not careful. Rank the various priorities, list pros and cons, and manipulate your general conception to try to achieve the least disruption and loss. Remember that a sensitively planned patio will often enhance the whole garden and can be sited anywhere on the plot – in its farthest corner, for example, instead of the more obvious position adjacent to the house.

The basement climate

Whereas larger courtyards are often sun traps, smaller yards, passageways and sunken 'areas' may be permanently shaded, at least at ground level. Cool moist air tends to settle here, providing welcome relief in hot weather but remaining cold, even frozen, longer than elsewhere in winter. Use warm floor materials, bright colours, reflective materials and robust shade-tolerant plants to green these spaces; try to admit ventilation to relieve lingering dampness; and add patio heating and lighting to improve the psychological as well as physical atmosphere.

The disaster area With derelict and overgrown gardens you need to decide whether there are any features worth preserving – paths and structures, perhaps, a neglected shrub or tree, or an abandoned pond – or whether clearing the ground and starting again might be the more satisfying and cost-effective option (see page 22). Before choosing where to build, wait up to a year for an unfamiliar old garden to reveal any hidden or dormant treasures and critical information like the sunniest places or a seasonal frost hollow.

No garden You might be starting with a concrete courtyard or basement area, a balcony or roof site, or even a houseboat or corner of an adjacent car park. Since a patio may be whatever size or shape you choose, it can be tailored to fit virtually any site or purpose, and provide you with enough room for at least a chair and a few potted plants. You might have to cope with exceptional circumstances like high winds at rooftop level or the sunless damp conditions of a site below ground (see box), but nothing is insuperable.

Make-over principles

When considering the renovation of a derelict site, plan the work in the following distinct stages:

Enhancement Weigh up which existing areas might be salvaged or modified to preserve any good points that can be integrated in the new scheme.

Elimination Clearing specific places may have dramatic results – removing a diseased tree or shrub, for example, or moving utilitarian areas like dustbins and washing lines.

Addition Building a new path or patio and installing lighting and water can all improve the context of existing features without further major change.

ASSESSING THE SITE

You should note any more obvious virtues or defects early on while there is still time to decide whether construction is feasible and where.

It is best to consider the most obvious first: do you actually like, or will you grow to like, being outdoors in the chosen spot? Almost any environmental intrusion can be

Concrete or reconstituted stone slabs may be inset in turf like stepping stones to make a subtly integrated surface (left) or butted together as a seamless and maintenance-free pavement (right).

ameliorated, if not entirely removed, whether it is an unwelcome noise or view, but in some circumstances the happiest solution might be compromise. For example, if sitting outside is not a total joy, you could build a patio next to the house or on a balcony and devote it entirely to plants and landscape accessories like stones and water to enjoy from indoors. Although originally intended for the pleasure and comfort of people, a patio does not have to be populated to succeed.

If your garden is very limited in size, there might be little freedom of choice about where to site the patio, and in a courtyard, balcony or rooftop garden the position and alignment is often decided for you. In a larger garden, however, there is usually more latitude, and a number of factors could then influence your decision or suggest changes that need to be made to help the design fit into its surroundings.

Planning a patio as an outdoor gathering place can exploit the most extreme site, from city panorama at roof level (left) to a front-row seat at the ocean's edge (right). In both situations timber excels as a tough, adaptable and lightweight flooring material.

Xerophytes

These are plants that can withstand hot dry conditions, usually because they come from regions with this kind of climate. With their inbuilt resilience and low-maintenance needs they make excellent patio plants, but if the patio is likely to experience frost make sure that the species you choose are also hardy. Suitable subjects include most Mediterranean, Australian and Californian shrubs, succulents and cacti; drought-resistant herbaceous plants such as echinops, eryngiums and euphorbias; and many bulbs, especially alliums, crocuses, muscaris, almost all tulips and most South African bulbs.

Aspect Note whether the site is predominantly sunny or shaded, and when it is in full sun. This will affect your comfort whenever you are most likely to be using the patio, and also determine the kind of plants that will thrive easily there. If the site is exposed to full sun, many plants could suffer unless watered frequently and lavishly (see box). Consider whether you might be able to modify the aspect, for example with screening or by thinning a nearby tree.

Shelter Find where the prevailing winds come from and test if this might be a source of discomfort. Draughts funnelling between buildings can be deflected or filtered, or you might prefer to construct a more substantial enclosure in an exposed position. This need not dominate or exclude light if you use climbers or wall shrubs trained like a lean hedge on trellis, or perhaps a wall built from glass bricks.

A typically stark passageway between buildings (left) has been transformed into a stylish courtyard by introducing bold seating, flooring and planting structures, while the equally uncluttered lines of a simple timber platform and access steps (right) shape a calm oasis in a verdant corner of an established garden.

Views Make sure you like what you will see while sitting on the patio. A screen or strategic planting can disguise an eyesore, while pruning or removing plants that obscure a view could allow you to 'borrow' the landscape beyond as part of the picture. Remember that the composition will include the sky, the view of which might be compromised if you plan an awning or bamboo pole roof, for example, or a sliding glass roof over a courtyard.

Surroundings Will the patio blend imperceptibly into its setting, enhance it or dominate features that are important? Any change produces ripples throughout its wider context, and a major structure like a patio will cause readjustment in the overall feeling of balance. Deliberately enclosing the patio as a walled room might be more successful than an uneasy coexistence with the rest of the garden.

Levels Not all gardens are made on the level, and you may have to accommodate a gradient. Far from being a problem, this can suggest exciting opportunities for split-level surfaces, perhaps with raised beds, terraces, steps and tumbling water features. Define the changes of level with contrasting floor materials to identify corridors and gathering places, enjoy any views from seating at the top and exploit lower levels for sunken gardens.

A sample of the many possible floor materials for a patio or courtyard – gravel, stone blocks, riven paving slabs, even lawn turf – each with distinctive visual and textural qualities that merit consideration.

The hidden level

A patio close to the house or linked to it may lie over one or more of the underground mains services: electricity, gas, water or oil supplies into the building, and drains leading away from it. To avoid damaging these while digging foundations, find out where they are and make sure that they are accessible at all times after the project is finished.

Property deeds sometimes include a plan of these services, or the public utility concerned may be able to tell you or your contractor. Lifting manholes and inspection covers will often reveal the course of a service, and above-ground connections can also indicate its position.

Patio sites away from the house will usually be on relatively undisturbed ground where it is safe for you to build, although it is always advisable to check first.

Drainage

Any hard floor over the soil impedes natural drainage and creates a new watershed. For this reason large areas of non-porous material are laid with a gentle slope or camber to discharge surface water, which can be collected at a drain or encouraged to run away harmlessly into an adjacent part of the garden (see also raised beds, page 97).

Rather than treat rainwater as a nuisance, try using it for practical or ornamental purposes.

Slope the patio subtly towards island beds or soil-filled joints in its surface to benefit plants and reduce the need for watering.

Guide surface water to a shallow gully or channel partly filled with pebbles or glass mulching material around or meandering across the patio as a water feature.

Lead surface water to a pond beside or within the patio, and supplement this with rainwater from the roof, collected in a butt with its overflow linked to your pond.

When you are satisfied that you have considered all the obvious qualities and possibilities of the site, you are almost ready to start. All that remains is to calculate a budget (and keep to it), break the project down into manageable stages and decide whether to hire contractors or do the work yourself.

2

PLANNING and BUILDING

With a dream now taking shape in your mind, it's time to come back to earth – literally, because you need to look at the potential site more closely and to consider whether the style and details you have set your heart on can work together successfully in the chosen position. This is an opportunity to explore the host of exciting materials and accessories available to help you create a practical and pleasing design that meets your needs and complements the patio's setting.

MAKING A START

THE ESSENTIAL STAGES

Draw up a plan

Measure the site as precisely as you can (a 30m/100ft surveyor's tape is useful for this) and transfer your figures to a plan of the garden drawn to scale on a sheet of squared paper; if preparing drawings to submit for planning consent, you will need to be very exact. Confirm the dimensions of square and rectangular shapes by measuring and matching their diagonal lengths. Draw in all the existing features – such as trees, walls, paths, manholes – and add the more important details of your design.

Mark out the site

When you are satisfied and ready to start, transfer the patio plan to the ground, marking out its essential lines and details with string tied to canes or pegs, or wrapped round bricks and stretched taut. Use sand or a spray marker to indicate curves. Check again that you approve the layout, and visualize its effect on the rest of the garden.

Prepare the site

All brick and slab surfaces need a firm and stable foundation to insulate them from changes in the soil below and traffic above. Skim off any turf with a spade

The most satisfying plans evolve from assessing the site as a whole, whether it is a small courtyard for resurfacing and planting (previous pages) or a scheme to pave paths and seating areas from one end of a garden to the other.

(stack this to rot for compost or re-use around the garden), and dig out the top 15cm (6in) or so of topsoil over the whole area (save this for filling raised beds or adding to potting mixtures). Level the excavated surface and tamp it firm with a heavy post or a hired plate compacter. Check levels and slopes, and then prepare the base (see box).

A base for paving

- If laying on sand: spread, level and compact a 10cm (4in) layer of hardcore or crushed stone, topped with 5–8cm (2–3in) of level, firmed dry sand over the whole area.
- If laying in mortar: prepare a hardcore bed as above, and cover with a 10mm (1/2in) bed of dry sand to leave a level surface. Mix and pour a 2.5cm (1in) layer of mortar, enough to bed 3–4 slabs at a time.

With care flooring materials can be mixed successfully, as here (left), where a drift of gravel encircles an island of paving slabs like a dry moat. Weathered materials like worn brick, however, often reveal so much character that they deserve to star as a solo feature (right).

THE PATIO FLOOR

A major component of any patio or courtyard is the finished flooring material. Almost certainly the most expensive element in your scheme, this needs to be strong and durable, and properly installed on a sound and well-drained foundation. The type you choose will depend on a number of factors, such as appearance, cost, ease of laying and the amount of wear it is likely to get. There are three main types of surfacing material: pavers, such as stone slabs or bricks; timber decking; and loose aggregates such as gravel and slate chippings.

PATIO PAVING

Stone, concrete and brick are all rigid and durable materials for areas of heavy use, provided they are bedded on a firmly consolidated base course (see box page 33). They are easy to lay, if you are doing the work yourself, and to maintain.

The even and consistent finish of interlocking stone slabs carefully laid on a sound foundation makes a safe level deck for dining furniture.

Paving slabs

These may be cast in concrete or reconstituted stone, in a range of colours that fade and soften with age, or cut from natural stone, often with a textured or riven finish. Baked terracotta tiles are also available in warm mellow shades. All have crisp clean outlines and come in various sizes, allowing you to lay interesting patterns. Larger sizes can be very heavy to handle, so manoeuvre them with care and wear heavy-duty gloves. Recycled flagstones may vary in thickness. Broken slabs are inexpensive and the traditional material for 'crazy paving', but need skilful arrangement to achieve a pleasing random finish.

Bricks and setts

Smaller paving units need more time and care to lay evenly but have greater design potential, whether on their own in a variety of geometric patterns or in conjunction with slabs, as highlights, inserts or edging. New and recycled bricks, with their classic rustic colours and finish, should be frost-proof to avoid crumbling or flaking. Granite and sandstone setts are extremely hard and

Where the patio will be conspicuous from a height there is an additional reason to compose a pleasing design using decorative units such as floor tiles, setts or bricks.

Building tips

- If joints are mortared to produce an impervious finish, the patio floor should have a gentle slope to shed surface water. Aim for a fall of about 1cm per metre (½in per yard) *away* from walls and buildings and *towards* a drain or pond.
- Make sure the finished surface is at least 15cm (6in) or two brick courses below the damp-proof course of house walls to avoid problems with moisture being absorbed into the building.
- Omit occasional slabs or pavers if you want to expose soil for planting or to accommodate a water feature or fire pit. Mortar joints can be filled with soil here and there for prostrate pavement plants.
- Experiment with lines of small paving stones like bricks and blocks to deceive the eye and 'stretch' the patio's shape in the direction in which they run.

With their workability and relatively low weight, timber boards are the ideal material on balconies and rooftops for decking, edging and (left) even for cladding a hot tub.

weather-resistant, with a slightly rounded profile better suited to paths and edgings than main seating areas (furniture needs even surfaces for stability).

WOODEN DECKING

While not as durable as stone or brick, good-quality seasoned timber will last for many years with a little routine care. It is comparatively light and very attractive, blends sympathetically with its surroundings, and is easily fashioned into a range of shapes and structures. Decking is bought as long, smooth or fluted planks of various widths or in pre-formed 'tiles' up to 1m (39in) square.

Hardwoods like oak, teak, karri and iroko are dense and heavy. Although expensive, they are naturally durable, with rich appealing colours that are easily preserved with annual treatment or can be left to weather to a soft silvery patina. Decay-resistant softwoods like western red cedar behave in the same way.

Other softwoods such as pine and fir are light and easy to work, with a pale finish that is often enhanced by

Left Boards sold for decking can also be used for constructing fences and partitions, where they blend in easily by day or artificial light.
Right Some boards have a ridged or fluted finish to improve drainage and provide a safer all-weather surface under foot.

painting with a natural or coloured wood stain. They can quickly deteriorate from wear and weathering unless pressure-treated with preservative, which will often extend their life from five to twenty-five years or more. Further regular rot-proofing is advisable.

Building decking

The surface boards are nailed or screwed to a framework of 15 by 5cm (6 by 2in) joists, set on edge about 38cm (15in) apart. These rest on concrete blocks on an existing hard surface or concrete foundation. Over soil the joists can be screwed or bolted to 10cm (4in) square posts, each set on a concrete block in a hole about 30cm (12in) deep and wide, which is then filled with concrete. Build raised decks or terraces on similar upright posts locked into spiked post-holders driven into the ground. All timber should be pressure-treated with preservative.

Timber care

- Choose boards at least 5cm (2in) thick to combat warping from temperature and moisture changes.

Buying decking

In many parts of the world timber cutting and consumption exceeds replanting, and indiscriminate felling of many kinds – especially some tropical hardwoods – is endangering long-term supplies. Check that the timber you buy is labelled as originating from sustainably managed forests. Some preservative treatments use potentially toxic chemicals, but environmentally friendly alternatives are available.

Cobbles, gravel and larger rocks are natural materials that look effective as an artless detail within and around a main structure (left) as well as making a vital traditional landscape ingredient of Oriental designs (right).

- Leave 5–10mm (¼–½in) expansion spaces between boards to allow them to swell after rain.
- Slightly roughen boards with sand or a wire brush to forestall slipperiness in wet weather.
- Seal all timber with a water-repellent preservative every two to three years for long life.

LOOSE AGGREGATES

While not recommended for the main patio floor, loose stone aggregates have huge decorative and landscaping potential, adding texture and contrast as infills, surface patterns and edgings. Recycled materials like glass gravel and metal granules can be spread loose over a weed-suppressant membrane for small areas of bold colour, especially in contemporary and minimalist schemes; bedded in mortar or resin they set as a tough and durable paving surface. Stone fragments are available in a range of sizes, texture and colours, from naturally subtle to vividly dyed in daring and flamboyant shades.

Indulge your creative instincts by experimenting with shapes and combinations of these versatile materials as local accents, or use a favourite for a main ingredient of your design. Choose pale materials to relieve shade and dark or sombre paving. Remember to confine loose materials with edging to prevent scatter, and increase their depth or foundation in heavily used areas.

Types of aggregate

Pebbles and cobbles Large stones of various kinds, generally smooth and water-worn. Pebbles are flatter and good for spreading loose, whereas cobbles are very rounded and best bedded in mortar.

Gravel and shingle Smaller stone fragments of various materials – either in mixed colours and minerals or

Gravel, shingle and similar loose aggregates are the perfect medium in which to grow plants, but may be easier to negotiate underfoot if inset with more solid slabs and tiles as stepping stones (left).

uniform – and generally in the range 0.5–2cm (¼–¾in) diameter. Gravel is irregular, while shingle is finer and more rounded.

Chippings and granules The smallest fragments, again mixed or a single mineral, and available in various hues, either natural (as in types of slate) or dyed.

Glass and metal Innovative materials for paving and mulching. Glass gravel is rounded, polished and comes in different colours. Metal granules are recycled copper or aluminium fragments, which are bright and angular in appearance.

Edgings for aggregates

Decide first whether the edging is to be an integral part of the design or purely functional and discreet. Various kinds of lawn edging strips, old slates or treated gravel boards for fencing, held in place by pegs, are ideal for simple or invisible frames. In more conspicuous positions use frost-proof bricks, decorative terracotta tiles, stone setts bedded in mortar, reclaimed railway sleepers or man-made materials such as cast concrete units, zinc or aluminium sheeting for stronger visual impact.

Buying aggregates

- Although a builders' merchant can calculate quantities from your measurements, it is useful to have a rough idea at the planning stage, especially when costing the work.
- Gravel, cobbles and pebbles: sold by the cubic metre or yard; expect 1 cu.m to cover 40 sq.m at 2.5cm (1in) depth, and 1cu.yd to cover 36sq.yd.
- Decorative aggregates: sold by the 25kg (56lb) bag, which will cover about 1 sq.m (just over 1 sq.yd) at 2.5cm (1in) deep.

OTHER MATERIALS

Parts of the floor can be given special treatment that will fuse pattern, texture and colour into exciting local highlights. This is particularly effective where the main material has a muted or subtler finish.

Metal is a sleek, reflective material, cold underfoot but versatile and sophisticated when used for detail or emphasis in your design. Copper ages to a mellow lustre; aluminium and stainless steel remain cool and bright; and

mild steel rusts in glorious autumnal shades. Use them in strips or sheets for edgings and outlines, as grilles over water or for interplanting with mats of tiny foliage, or recycled as mulching granules (see aggregates).

Mosaics can be made from small pieces of almost any weather-resistant material, from treated slices of logs incorporated into decking designs to pebbles, slate fragments, broken china or manufactured tesserae set in mortar. You can glean inspiration from a range of natural and fine art sources, and produce inventive designs to embellish a patio or courtyard floor with centrepieces, focal points or ribbons of colour, or even breathe new life into a bland existing surface by covering it with a full-size mosaic like an ornate carpet.

Mosaic components such as glass and stone fragments (above) or pebbles in various shapes and shades (below) can be set in concrete to add a durable and divergent flourish to any paving scheme.

FRAMING THE PATIO

As a clearly separate space, the patio has distinct edges – a flowerbed between paving and lawn, for example, or the walls and buildings around an enclosed courtyard. These margins are an important practical and aesthetic part of the design and may need careful consideration before you lay the floor itself.

Even if you want the patio to merge imperceptibly into the rest of the garden, the surfacing materials you choose will usually need some kind of permanent edge restraint, especially if bedded on sand. Special stone or concrete strips or bricks can be mortared around the perimeter, or you can use treated timber edging boards nailed or screwed to strong 5cm- (2in-) square pegs.

More substantial boundaries can play an active role in determining the character of the design, creating strong visual definition or adding extra qualities such as shelter and privacy. Walls can be built from a variety of materials, and range in size from a couple of courses of concrete screen blocks or a low double wall filled with soil and small plants, up to 2m (6½ft) fence or trellis panels to deflect wind or screen an eyesore. Taller walls need deep

A simple fence of posts and ropes adds a sense of enclosure and security without obscuring the wider garden setting.

A boundary may be a token definition of place (left) or a more substantial screen (right) that confers shelter and privacy on the patio.

foundations and possibly pillars for reinforcement, while fence and trellis panels are supported by sturdy posts and sometimes linking rails.

Assess the impact of a proposed boundary from both sides to make sure that it does not take up too much of the garden or have an adverse effect on its surroundings, such as casting shade, causing wind turbulence or demeaning nearby features.

Entrances and exits

Raised and enclosed patios need some kind of access to and from the garden; even an open-sided structure away from the house or a pocket-size patio in a small corner will usually be reached by a path. This is the chance to make a bold or inviting feature, depending on the atmosphere you want to create. Plants in formal pots could flank the entrance like sentinels, or you could use coloured pebbles, paddlestones or glass beads set in mortar to make a mosaic threshold. Explore unusual materials, and with a little imagination this important focal point can be something special.

Boundary ideas

- A low-cavity brick wall capped with a water trough for a canal of still water.
- A single rail of rope or poles – even stone for grandeur – to make a formal terrace or balcony.
- Inexpensive concrete blocks, rendered with polished cement for a contemporary finish or with rough painted limewash in adobe style.
- A cordwood wall made from assorted log sections, stacked on their sides and mortared together with their endgrain visible.
- An earth bank built with turves stripped from the patio site and planted with wild flowers and herbs.

Modular panels (left) supply instant walls for colour and as a backdrop to plantings, while even the plainest brick wall (right) can become an active part of the scheme when embellished with painted trellis and a mirror strategically placed as a *trompe-l'oeil* to reflect part of the distant landscape.

Depending on the finished height above ground level you may need to build one or two steps for access. These can be made from timber to match wooden decking, or from the same paving materials set on brick or block risers. For comfort and safety steps are usually 10–15cm (4–6in) high, while the depth of the treads should be at least 30cm (12in) from front to back. Make sure that the steps are wide enough – 90–120cm (3–4ft) may not be over-generous – and in scale with the rest of the patio.

Existing walls

House and garden walls next to a patio or around courtyards may present a challenge if they are not to dominate or overshadow the site. Depending on their style and condition, you should be able to incorporate them as an extra dimension in the design.

Simply painting a wall may be enough to improve its visual merit, especially in a dull or sunless position where two to three coats of white masonry paint or limewash will reflect extra light and even add a Mediterranean air to the site. Bright flowering plants in hanging pots or on shelves

can relieve any uniformity. Regular repainting will be necessary, however, which might mean disturbing plants trained on the walls, and it may be preferable to accept the wall's natural finish as a neutral background for plants or more decorative structures.

Mirrors are often used successfully to reflect light and produce an impressive illusion of more space, especially if combined with the reflective properties of a water feature installed near by. *Trompe l'oeil* is a method of distorting perspective to suggest greater size or distance by painting or constructing a fake scene, such as a view through a door, window or archway. Narrow soil-filled beds or troughs at the foot of a wall allow climbers to embellish and redeem the most unappealing surface.

The patio roof

The most obvious and, many would argue, most appropriate roof for any patio or courtyard is the sky itself, with its ever-changing colours and moods. In high summer, though, the sun's direct heat may be overwhelming, while sudden rainfall can interrupt festivities any time unless there is some kind of overhead protection.

A free-standing parasol may provide sufficient shade and shelter, or a canvas canopy can be slung like a nomad's tent and attached with ropes to handy trees or wall fixings. A more permanent solution might be a retractable awning fitted to a high wall; a pergola or gazebo frame decked with climbing plants for dappled shade (and possibly strung with lights for evening

An outdoor living space need not merge unobtrusively into its garden surroundings, and can be successfully emphasized by the daring use of sophisticated structures (left) or vibrant colour (right).

Using trellis

This is more adaptable than might be assumed from the standard panels built with a square or diamond grid for training plants, and you can often dismantle and rearrange the slim wooden strips to create your own wall designs. The ancient art of treillage used this versatile material to fashion battlements, fanciful towers and architectural follies, often painted and used as plant supports or as airy structures in their own right. Instead of timber you could use copper tubing, bamboo, willow, or mild steel strip or mesh.

conviviality); a simple porch or arbour over an individual seat, covered with plants for shade or with a more waterproof material like thatch or tiles for shelter from rain.

COLOUR

Flowering plants were traditionally used as the main source of colour in the garden, but contemporary designers have broken with this custom and a multitude of exterior paints, stains and finishes is now available to decorate virtually any surface and transform the hard finish of built structures. These need to be used with care: bold blocks of primary colours may be stimulating in a simple

Patio palette – the effect of colours

- Blue: a soothing, healing colour that complements green foliage.
- Gold: adds exotic hints, especially in themed Oriental gardens.
- White: a sparkling finish, best for reflecting light and relieving gloom.
- Grey: calm and refreshing, and flatters flower colours.
- Dark green: crisp and formal, a good foil for other shades.
- Yellow: warm and comforting, but needs good daylight.
- Red: variously festive, imperious or sumptuous – use with care.

or minimalist design, but can easily dominate the garden and its contents. It is often more effective to concentrate on subdued colours – the various greens of plant foliage and the natural shades of stone, brick and timber, for example – and rely on furniture, painted containers and smaller decorative features like sculpture or inlays of metal and glass marbles to supply brilliant highlights.

Weather-resistant paint ranges suggest a host of colours for use outdoors: your choice might blend into the rest of the garden (right) or stand out in exciting contrast (far right).

LIGHTING

Including artificial lighting in the patio decor can completely alter its character, allowing you to enjoy the hours after sundown and adding a touch of enchantment or drama to the setting. The display can be as basic or elaborate as you wish, from a tiny fleet of café lights floating in a dish of water to a fully choreographed sequence of fibre optics. Choose with restraint: the best lighting effects are subtle and unobtrusive, whereas too much light easily dispels the charm and intimacy of alfresco evenings on the patio.

It is important to distinguish between the two main functions of outdoor lighting.

Whether used to illuminate this decorative wall panel (left) or the clustered stems of specimen plants (right), artificial lighting is a dynamic accessory for creating atmosphere and drama with its play of shadow and silhouette.

Primary lighting This is essentially functional, installed for safety, security or convenience. It may consist of floodlights that bathe large areas in strong light triggered, perhaps, by an intruder sensor, or spotlights with focused beams for smaller targets like steps, a barbecue or a hazardous corner. Solar spikes store power by day to illuminate paths and patio edges after dark.

Lighting safety

- Electricity is dangerous outdoors. Always get a qualified electrician to install a mains supply to waterproof power points.
- Minimize risks by choosing low-voltage equipment connected to the mains via a transformer.
- Fit an RCD (circuit breaker) at the main socket to cut the current in the event of an accident.
- Use strong weatherproof cable and sturdy supports when mounting lamps.
- Shield flares, candles and other naked flames from wind, and use well away from flammable materials.

Secondary lighting This is used for entertainment or aesthetic impact, to create moods, mystery or a play of light and shadow. Spotlights concealed under water or beneath plants as uplighters are a simple way to achieve these effects, while fibre-optic devices can be installed in the patio floor, in trees or twined along trellis for playful colour and sparkle.

WATER

Water is an active as much as a decorative element in the garden. Depending on how you use it in your design, it can brood, glimmer or fill the air with freshness

Platforms of timber decking provide safe access as well as an appropriate setting for a hot tub that doubles as a garden pool.

and sound. Imaginative gardeners have enclosed a patio like an island with a shallow moat, led rippling canals across the surface or along walls, built a deck over illuminated still pools, and even piped rainwater to chuckle its way down gullies and into overflowing basins. Water is a life force that can animate the patio scene in many unique ways.

Plan any features at an early stage because you may need to allow for pipes to supply and conduct electricity if you install a pump, or possibly leave space for sunken containers such as a half-barrel for a pool or separate foundations for a hot tub.

Options

Still water Even a tiny pool can mirror the sky, twinkle with light and cool the air as it evaporates, all of which add personality to a patio environment. Disperse bowls on tables and other surfaces for use as birdbaths and for floating candles and flower heads. Tucked among plants or perhaps raised within knee-high walls, shallow pools and bowls reflect foliage and reinforce flower scents. You

Water know-how

- Just 5–8cm (2–3in) of standing water can be dangerous to very young children, so limit designs to gentle fountains or trickles over stones if they play near by.
- Water and electricity are a potentially lethal team. Have moving water features installed or checked by a qualified electrician.
- Fit an RCD (circuit breaker) to electric pumps and service these annually; disconnect and store them indoors in cold winters.

Water can be introduced into designs as a focal point, as in this unpretentious stone sphere and bubble fountain (left); the more elaborate stony stream (right) adds lively sound, movement and a play of light to the patio environment.

could make a larger pond as a focal point or wildlife haven in a planted corner, using a pre-cast container or a simple dished depression lined with mortar and embedded stones.

Flowing water By installing a surface or submersible pump, you can circulate water from a reservoir through lively devices such as a fountain jet, a gush of bubbles through pebbles or the centre of a millstone, or along a stream channelled across the patio floor to a reservoir pool. There is no need to drench the area: the shallowest film of moving water can add sound and life to its surroundings.

Falling water For a more vivacious spectacle, hide the delivery pipe under rocks or behind plants to exit at a height and flow along a rill, trickle from a wall plaque or cascade down a series of bowls into a collecting pool. Again this does not have to be a torrent; even a gentle current will chatter merrily through a bamboo spout, along suspended chains or down the face of a mirror with impressive effect.

FURNITURE

To make the most of alfresco opportunities on the patio, choose a range of appropriate furniture to match the style and meet your needs, whether these are for occasional quiet relaxation or lavish entertaining. Remember that all the items need to be weatherproof and easily maintained, unless you can store them under cover, away from rain and frost.

Preliminary thoughts

Consider how many people need seating, and how much space is available for any permanent arrangement of furniture.

Tables and chairs can be lightweight and collapsible for moving round, or heavy and fixed, perhaps doubling as chests or storage containers.

Permanent seating is best sited where there is a pleasing view, possibly with shade from the midday heat but catching the rising or setting sun for quieter moments.

Make sure that furniture, especially lightweight items, is stable and that there is enough of a level surface to set them out safely.

Plan ample space for people to move round comfortably, especially where there are also plant containers and accessories like sunshades, heaters and lights.

As long as it is weatherproof and easily maintained, patio furniture is a matter for personal choice, and comes in styles that range from unadorned solid timber (left) for more rustic settings to the airy elegance of metal street café items (below).

Careful selection may be necessary to distinguish furniture that might be appropriate for formal dining (left) from designs better suited to more homely activities such as family teas and afternoon siestas (right).

Consider divergent solutions: tables and seats can be built into walls; scattered cushions, beanbags and inflatables make good emergency seating; a hammock can be the most enticing lounger of all.

Materials

Wood Always the least intrusive material, this looks warm, natural and inviting, and can be used in a variety of styles. As with decking, hard- and softwoods vary in price, quality and durability. All may be stained or painted, sealed or left to weather naturally.

Metal Hard-wearing, very long-lasting and often inexpensive, this can be stark and contemporary with a coloured or polished finish, or heavy and traditional – for instance ornate wrought iron finished in black paint.

Cane Together with similar materials like bamboo, willow and hazel, this is elegant and strong, with a hint of faraway times and places. It is light and durable, especially if treated regularly against rot and wood beetles.

Plastic Inexpensive, unsophisticated but sometimes the most comfortable, and long-lasting if resistant to ultra violet light. Most items are easily moved and stacked, and can usually be left out all year.

HEATING AND EATING

In cooler climates the season for comfortable outdoor living may seem disappointingly transitory, but various heating options can help keep the cold at bay.

Although bulky and expensive, gas-powered standard heaters can supply overhead light as well as warmth over a large area. A metal or pottery chiminea is a more elegant solution, originally from Mexico and fuelled by wood or charcoal to give a live fire for heating and cooking. Dished metal braziers are a modern version of the humdrum incinerator. A fire pit of bricks and mortar sunk in the ground offers the warmth and romance of a bonfire combined with safety and (if fitted with a grille) alfresco cooking facilities.

BARBECUES

For ease and convenience, a barbecue is the most efficient method of cooking outdoors. A range of types is available.

Disposable Simplest and least expensive: a foil tray filled with charcoal and covered with a wire or metal grille.

Including space for permanent or seasonal cooking facilities such as this stylish and sophisticated barbecue (right) completes arrangements for alfresco dining.

Portable Wheeled or collapsible models, often smartly designed; readily stored out of the way when not needed.

Built-in Permanent DIY structures of brick or stone, with a solid hearth or fire cradle and cooking grille or spit.

Be fire-wise

- Flames and smoke are hazardous, so shield fires from wind, and keep children, flammable materials and fire-lighting equipment well away from each other.
- Smoke and cooking smells are anti-social nuisances: choose still weather for cooking outdoors or site the barbecue downwind of neighbours.
- Wear protective clothing near fire, keep extinguishers such as water and sand near by, and make sure that fires are completely out after use.

3

PLANTING the PATIO

Plants are a joy in their own right, as every gardener knows. In the hard-edged, geometric setting of a patio or courtyard, however, they bring more than just supplementary colour and variety: as an adaptable and dynamic ingredient they can make a fundamental contribution to the vitality of your plan. With tactical choice and placing, just a few appropriate specimens will supply height, texture and seasonal change, while more lavish plantings can transform the whole atmosphere of an otherwise plain space.

CONSIDERING PLANTS

Although plants might make a garden for most people, a patio need not depend on them for success. A pleasing composition of elegant lines and attractive materials, especially in an urban setting of roofs, walls and buildings, may be sufficient or require only a token number of outstanding plants as special accents.

Plants are more than just soft furnishing, though: they can deflect wind, confer privacy, filter hot sunlight, and cool or perfume the air, for example. They are remarkably successful at improving air quality in town gardens, trapping up to 85 per cent of gases and particles on their leaves, from which rain then washes the pollutants safely into the soil. Climbers and wall shrubs can protect the fabric of courtyard walls and insulate house walls from extreme cold and heat.

Plants that tolerate pollution

Easily grown plants with notable tolerance of urban pollution include buddlejas, calendula, cotoneasters, lavatera, hollyhocks, maples, mock oranges, olearia, pelargoniums, periwinkles, petunias, robinia, saxifrages, syringa, tulips and viburnums.

Plants are added to the patio scene in a host of ways, whether as specimen flowers like heat- and sun-loving bougainvilleas (left) and fragrant French lavender (*Lavandula stoechas*, right) or as a crowded cottage garden collection of flamboyant perennials and annuals (previous pages).

One of the less obvious qualities of plants is their ability to settle any built structure into a context of change and natural cycles. A bare patio or courtyard looks much the same at any time of year, whereas plants register the seasons. A patio may be striking but need not be sterile.

Composing small pictures

If you have just built a new patio, take another look at the finished design before choosing any plants and remind yourself of your earlier planting ideas (see Chapter 1). These may change now that you can appreciate the reality of the area and its impact on the surroundings. You might want to reconsider those preliminary thoughts, explore new options and revise any draft plant lists to complement the size and style of the patio.

Whether you decide to grow a few specimens as stylish highlights or to green whole areas of the patio with sumptuous plantings, the range of potential plants may be bewildering and the amount of available space impossibly small. Any perceived problem may be turned to advantage, however.

Decide early in the planning stage whether plants are to be grown and staged in containers (left) or as permanent occupants of integrated beds (right) – often the more successful option for large or vigorous subjects.

Adjust your focus In a limited space every plant needs to work hard to merit inclusion. Instead of planting in colonies and drifts, try choosing distinctive individual plants with special qualities, and get to know them intimately around the seasons. If they become indispensable favourites, keep them, but replace any that disappoint or become commonplace.

Integrate plants vertically Natural systems like woodlands often comprise three layers or storeys: a top canopy of trees, a middle storey of shrubs and a ground layer of herbaceous plants. This arrangement balances competing needs, shares out resources and maximizes the diversity of plants in a given area.

Identify similarities Although the apparently artless muddle of a cottage garden has its appeal, it is easier to manage in an open garden than in a small patio space, where organizing plants according to their needs is often more practical. Grow sun-lovers in the brightest part, and underplant with shade-lovers or grow these in

The warm shelter and free drainage of an enclosed gravel patio scheme supplies the perfect protected environment for this excitingly colourful gathering of New Zealand flax (*Phormium*) cultivars.

Plants to cut hard

Coppicing is the practice of cutting trees and shrubs at regular intervals almost to ground level. This controls size, rejuvenates growth and often enhances their special qualities – plants with coloured stems and ornamental foliage respond particularly well. You can alternate the treatment on two specimens of a variety to ensure an uninterrupted display. Plants to coppice to about 15cm (6in) high every other year or so include *Buddleja davidii*, coloured forms of *Cornus alba* and *Salix alba*, eucalyptus (especially *E. gunnii*), purple or golden hazels and elders, sumachs and ailanthus (tree of heaven).

other less sunlit areas. Gather lime-hating plants in a special bed or large container of suitable compost and tender plants where they can be assembled for convenient protection.

Keep in trim With the exception of structural plants, save space by regularly cutting back top growth and splitting perennials that steadily fatten with age. Grow more vigorous plants in containers, where root confinement and division or root trimming at repotting time all help to restrict growth. Annual clipping to shape will restrain most shrubs and woody herbs, while some trees and shrubs benefit from regular hard pruning or coppicing (see box).

MATCHING THE MICROCLIMATE

The specific microclimate of a patio or courtyard is a blend of environmental influences – shade from trees, for example, still air trapped by surrounding buildings or the rain shadow effect of high walls – and conditions supplied by the structure itself, such as reflected heat from paving and high humidity from water features or lingering dampness.

Some of these conditions can be modified (see Chapter 1), or you can choose plants that will be content with things as they are. Plants have adapted to virtually every kind of habitat in the world, so it is not difficult to compile a selection of candidates that should thrive in your site's microclimate.

Plants for hot dry patios

- Succulents (such as aloes, sedums, sempervivums and yuccas).
- Silver/grey plants (artemisias, cistus, eryngiums, lavender).
- Aromatic herbs (oregano, rosemary, sages, thymes).
- Summer bedding (cosmos, dahlias, osteospermums, tagetes).
- Tender bulbs (agapanthus, eucomis, gladioli, nerines).
- Sun-loving fruits (figs, grapes, loquats, kiwi fruit).

In general, the patio climate is likely to benefit plants. Its greater warmth, shelter and humidity all favour growth, while variations in light and shade across the site, especially in enclosed yards, can extend the range of choice beyond that suited to the open garden environment. The main aim should be to match plant preferences to the prevailing conditions.

Sun and shade

The greatest influence on growth will probably be the amount of light or shade your plants are exposed to. At one extreme is the open patio linked directly to the sunny side of the house, where plants can revel in the

A thoughtful blend of water, terracotta, ochre-washed walls, diverse leaf forms and shades of green has transformed this sunny courtyard into a corner of a Mediterranean landscape.

extra absorbed warmth and undiluted sunlight – conditions that favour many variegated and less hardy varieties, succulents and tender summer bedding subjects. At the other is the enclosed sunken courtyard, where cool air lingers and the sun may only penetrate for part of the day, if at all. Here ferns, woodland flowers and bulbs, and many herbaceous foliage plants will be happy, together with large-leaved exotic plants for a rainforest theme.

Manipulating shade

Many plants (and some gardeners) cannot withstand uninterrupted hot sunshine without scorching or wilting, but there are ways to relieve the amount of exposure and so expand your potential planting choices.

Naturally small trees such as cherries, birches, dogwoods, maples and rowans have open deciduous canopies or can be pruned or trained accordingly to give dappled shade in the growing season. They will be happy and healthy for many years in large containers and can be underplanted with shade-lovers.

Shrubs and climbers such as hydrangeas (left) and fragrant roses (right) are key components in developing height and permanence in a planting scheme.

Climbers on screens, trellis panels and overhead frameworks can be deployed to cast soft shade at the hottest part of the day. If you choose deciduous species like most clematis and passionflowers, or annual climbers such as *Cobaea scandens*, sweet peas and runner beans, there will be no loss of light during the winter months when their foliage has died.

Where there is too much shade – more than half the day without sun can seriously limit your plant palette – you can admit more light by deploying reflective surfaces such as mirrors and areas of still water, painting walls, spreading pale or shiny ground-cover materials like crushed limestone or glass mulch, and by selective pruning.

Summer pruning (which does not stimulate more growth) can reduce the leaf canopy and punctuate the heavy shade it casts; or you can remove the lower branches of dense shrubs and conifers to turn them into standards with bare trunks and so admit more lateral light.

Shade-tolerant plants

- For moist shade: camellias, Japanese maples, daphnes, fatsia and hydrangeas (shrubs); hostas, dicentra, polygonatums, primulas, lily of the valley and many ferns (perennials); begonias, impatiens, mimulus and bluebells (annuals and bulbs).
- For dry shade: berberis, hazels, euonymus, skimmia and elders (shrubs); acanthus, bergenias, hellebores, pulmonaria and euphorbias (perennials); alliums, crocus, snowdrops, coleus, fuchsias and many annual grasses (annuals and bulbs).

STRUCTURAL PLANTS

The upper two storeys of natural plant communities – the tree and shrub layers – provide your composition with a permanent structure. Trees contribute shade, height and shelter, screen off or frame views, and add shape and pattern to the patio ceiling. Shrubs add colour and texture at eye level or below, defining or dividing spaces while adding bulk or background to herbaceous plants. Evergreen trees and shrubs can play a key role in winter when other plants are leafless (see box page 82).

You will probably have space for only one or two trees and a limited selection of shrubs, so these need to work hard and give value all year round. Lilacs, for example,

are gorgeous for a few weeks in spring while decked with fragrant blooms, but look very plain at other seasons, whereas the dogwood *Cornus alba* 'Elegantissima' entertains all year, with its cream and green foliage, broad heads of white flowers in summer followed by blue-tinted white berries, and vivid leaf tints in autumn.

Variegated or ornamental foliage is particularly colourful (often enhanced by hard pruning), as are autumn leaf tints, especially on exposed patios, where a combination of sunny autumn days and cold nights can produce a spectacular display. Deciduous species with coloured stems and young shoots or intriguingly contorted branches continue performing even when leafless. And don't forget fruit trees and bushes, outstanding for blossom and the bonus of fresh home-grown produce.

Key plants to consider

- Coloured bark and stems: birches, dogwoods, eucalyptus, *Fraxinus excelsior* 'Jaspidea', maples, *Prunus cerasifera*, willows.

- Variegated foliage: cultivars of acer, buddleja, ceanothus, cornus, cotoneaster, ilex, philadelphus, pyracantha, sambucus, viburnum and weigela.
- Branch structure: *Buddleja alternifolia*, corkscrew hazel and willow (*Corylus avellana* 'Contorta' and *Salix babylonica* var. *pekinensis* 'Tortuosa'), small weeping standards like *Salix caprea* 'Kilmarnock'.
- Winter fragrance: chimonanthus, corylopsis, daphne, elaeagnus, hamamelis, *Lonicera fragrantissima*, *Mahonia japonica*, *Viburnum carlesii*.

A patio is an ideal stage to set with compelling plant artistry such as container topiary and pleached trees (left) or for displaying whimsical conceits like living furniture (right).

Evergreens

- Evergreen shrubs, trees and conifers can improve any patio scheme by adding permanence and continuity through the seasonal changes of other plants. They are by no means changeless, though, and many bear attractive flowers or berries. Even the darkest conifer has its brighter moods when its fresh, often prettily coloured young foliage appears.
- Small evergreens for containers and patio beds include eucalyptus, variegated hollies, myrtle, pittosporum (trees); elaeagnus, hebes, laurels, olearia (shrubs); cryptomerias, *Juniperus horizontalis*, *Pinus mugo* cultivars, *Taxus baccata* 'Standishii' (conifers).

GREEN WALLS

Climbers are indispensable patio plants: they take up very little ground space and soon cloak large areas of wall or screen with attractive growth that can decorate a good design or disguise a blemish. They extend the growing

The walls of a courtyard are an extra planting dimension that invites use as a backdrop to a composition of shrubs (left), as support for climbers or even as a canvas for painted *trompe l'oeil* (right).

Cloaking the walls around a patio with flowering climbers helps cool the air on hot summer days and provides secure nesting sites for many garden birds.

area, filter dust, deaden sound and improve the patio climate by transpiring cooling water vapour into the air.

Some climbers are self-supporting; others need training to hold their stems in place and help them gain height.

Common ivy, Boston ivy and Virginia creeper use aerial roots to cling directly to any rough surface.

Clematis, grape vines and wisteria have spiralling stems or twining tendrils that need a grid of wires or strings attached to the wall with vine eyes (screw-in rings).

Wall shrubs like climbing roses, winter jasmine and flowering quinces have stiffer stems which are tied in to netting or wooden trellis screwed or bolted in place.

Always leave a 5–8cm (2–3in) space between the wall and climber supports for free air movement to combat dampness and disease.

THEMES AND MOODS

Soft herbaceous plants (the ground level of the three planting tiers) make up the largest and most adaptable group in the plant repertoire. You can use these to compose any miniature version of your favourite

Inspirations

- Consider planting directly into the joints of a garden wall, using plants like wallflowers, ferns, lewisias, stonecrops (*Sedum*) and ivy-leaved toadflax (*Cymbalaria muralis*). Wedge young plants into gaps with stones or clay, or mix seeds with moist compost and tamp in place.
- Match plants to the aspect. For sunny walls choose deciduous climbers such as clematis, climbing roses, jasmine and trumpet vine (*Campsis*); on cold, shaded walls use evergreens and native climbers, such as ivy, climbing hydrangea, honeysuckle and pyracantha.
- Climbers are favourite nesting and foraging habitats for birds like wrens, robins, thrushes and blackbirds. Best plants include native species – hops, old man's beard (*Clematis vitalba*) – and those with berries, such as cotoneaster and wild honeysuckle (*Lonicera periclymenum*).
- Many fruits are easily trained as climbers and espaliers on walls and free-standing supports, providing flower and fruit displays, nectar for bees and other insects, and strong nesting sites for birds. They include apples, pears, cherries, quinces, brambles, red and white currants, apricots and peaches, figs and grape vines.

gardening style – formal or informal, wildlife or historical – and as a decorative palette of colours to create a particular atmosphere on the patio.

A calm and satisfying monochrome display of evergreen foliage, all the more pleasing for being staged in a complementary landscape of pristine white walls and burnished terracotta floor tiles.

Colour themes

Using plants as a colour source is an established way to manipulate mood in the strong, often angular surroundings of walls and paving – for example, white and silver plants are cool and refreshing in summer, especially on hot patios, but may look distinctly chilly in winter. Compared to permanently painting or decorating the structure itself, plants are easier to establish, combine or replace, and to change with the seasons.

Greens Soothing and tranquil shades, ideal for relaxed and sunless sites. Green plants depend for impact mainly on their foliage, which can add contrast and shape, especially when lit at night. Try bold hostas, feathery fennel and marbled arums, punctuated with flowers like green varieties of euphorbia, nicotiana and zinnia.

Silver and white These are cool, almost insubstantial colours that sparkle in dappled shade and in the evening, but may seem washed out on a bright day and can even scorch in hot sunlight. Foliage plants like white-variegated forms of hostas, grasses and conifers can provide the basis of a collection, as can white-flowered spring bulbs, lilies, roses and dahlias (all good patio container plants).

Pastels Cool and calming without the austerity of white or green, and in a host of subtly different shades to blend together and tone down the midsummer sun. Blue, pink and lavender shades are restful, soft yellows and creams gentle and mellow. Deploy large-leaved foliage plants and climbers for a background and foil for pastel varieties of herbaceous perennials and seasonal annuals.

Hot colours Full sun and, very often, high temperatures are essential for reds, oranges, strong yellows and rich purples to work well. They add spice and animation to a patio, providing a vivacious setting for entertaining that often continues into autumn as summer flowers merge with the leaf tints of trees and shrubs. Annual summer bedding can supply some of the hottest shades for containers, baskets and sunny beds.

This emphatically geometric composition of rounded cobbles and precisely angular structures is reinforced by a collection of phormiums, each an explosion of strong linear evergreen foliage.

Exotic plants

With its extra shelter and warmth, a patio or courtyard can supply an ideal setting for hot-climate plants that might not survive or thrive in the open garden, and combining these with equally bold hardy plants would provide all the ingredients for a tropical paradise. Grow the frost-sensitive species in containers that can be moved under cover in winter, or be prepared to protect vulnerable stems and foliage with fleece or bubble wrap as insulation.

Compatible hardy plants include many bamboos, lush *Fatsia japonica*, palms like *Trachycarpus fortunei* or the cabbage tree *Cordyline australis*, and the evergreen *Drimys winteri* for background shelter. Add tender exotics such as olive, oleander, lemons, plumbago, bird of paradise (*Strelitzia*) and the borderline-hardy banana *Musa basjoo*. Houseplants such as aspidistra, maranta, rubber plants and bromeliads all benefit from a summer break outdoors and will supply authentic colour and texture.

Shingle and rock (far left) can be arranged to create a wild setting, while joints between paving slabs may be 'mortared' with sand or soil, to provide congenial planting niches (left). In both situations plants quickly spread and self-seed to produce a natural and established look.

More themes

- Oriental: lots of stone, wood, water and other natural materials, with a few choice specimen plants such as dwarf pines, Japanese maples, rhododendrons and cercidyphyllums growing in a carpet of moss. A sympathetic style for timber or gravel patios.
- Formal: symmetrical beds and arrangements of containers, laid out in a strongly geometrical pattern. Balance and discipline are important, together with neat plants such as topiary, clipped evergreen climbers and a limited number of restrained flowering plants. Ideal for a plaza effect in entertaining areas and front-garden patios.
- Wildlife: an informal, relaxed style, with the patio's outlines softened and obscured by profuse planting that supplies shelter for nesting sites, berries and out-of-season flowers for food, a pond to attract insects and aquatic creatures, and secluded seating for you to watch wildlife visitors.

Grapes (left) and figs, often grown together, are the classic fruits to train on an overhead framework, where they cast welcome shade for sitting in the midday sun.

PATIO PRODUCE

Growing your own does not require large areas of open ground, and a wide range of salads, herbs, vegetables and fruit can be produced in a patio garden without compromising its ornamental appearance. Most crops can be grown in containers and raised beds, some even in hanging baskets and window boxes, with plants arranged in traditional rows and blocks or in imaginative combinations with flowering plants. And the harvest will be fresh, tasty and near at hand for gathering.

Ground-level beds within or surrounding the patio can be used for utilitarian crops such as early potatoes or parsnips, and decorative vegetables like chard, curly kale and artichokes.

Runner beans, Japanese cucumbers and squashes are attractive rambling plants to train as climbers on wigwams, arches or trellis, perhaps mixed with sweet peas for fragrance.

Keep fresh salads and herbs close to the table, barbecue or back door where they can be picked at the last moment in peak condition; add nasturtiums and marigolds for colour and edible flowers.

Grow trained fruit for maximum yield in small spaces. Gooseberries, red currants and many tree fruits can be grown as espaliers, fans and cordons on walls and trellis, underplanted with lettuces and bedding plants.

Cordon, column and dwarf standard fruits are appealing in large containers, where you can also give blueberries their favourite acid compost; strawberries do well as edging, ground cover or in special strawberry towers.

Reserve the sunniest spots for tomatoes, peppers, aubergines and other heat-loving crops, in containers or a bed against a sunny wall.

WATER PLANTS

Some water features succeed without plants – simple canals, geysers and shallow pools, for example, where movement or clear reflection is their main purpose – while others are improved by plants or even require them to function well.

Most aquatic plants do not like fast currents or disturbance, and they are rarely happy near falling or swirling water, although you can always grow moisture-loving plants in a bog garden close by. Patio ponds are ideal sites, though, and can be planted for simplicity with a miniature water lily or, where there is the space and depth, with a wide selection of marginal and aquatic species. Wildlife ponds need a complete range of water plants dispersed around at least half the circumference and over about one-third of the surface.

Types of water plant

Deep-water aquatics These prefer a depth of at least 23cm (9in) and can cover a large surface area, so there is often room for only one or two specimens (usually a water lily). Attractive in any pond.

Floaters Unattached drifting species like water lettuce and water soldier, happiest in shallow water or bowls and neat enough for formal pools or table-top features.

Oxygenators Submerged plants that clean the water and keep it sweet. Important in larger pools and wildlife ponds for maintaining living conditions for fish and pond creatures.

Marginals Plants to grow near the edge of ponds with just their toes in the water. Irises, rushes and calla lilies are patio favourites, usually planted in submerged baskets for convenient maintenance.

Bog plants Often the easiest to accommodate, these simply need consistently moist but not waterlogged soil. Try growing rhubarb, rodgersia, day lilies or angels' fishing rods (*Dierama*) by water for stunning reflections.

PLACES FOR PLANTS

A bed of garden soil is undoubtedly the easiest place to grow plants: their roots are unrestricted and safe from freezing, there is less urgency about prompt watering and feeding, and they need no annual repotting.

Exposed soil can also balance the effects of the hard patio floor. Rainfall readily soaks in (whereas impervious surfaces increase peak runoff by about 50 per cent) and is then taken up by plants and evaporated through their leaves as cooling water vapour. Large areas of bare ground are unnecessary, and the same benefits apply even to joints and planting spaces between slabs, where plant roots can keep cool and search for the absorbed moisture.

CREVICE PLANTS

Some plants specialize in these restricted spaces, and enjoy the shaded root-run under slabs while their spreading top growth stays dry and warm on the surface above. Many crevice and pavement plants develop into neat mats or rounded cushions of tiny foliage that can shade the soil, suppressing weeds and embroidering the hard edges of paving units. Where whole slabs are left out, you could congregate prostrate plants in dense carpets like miniature lawns.

Dependable colonizers, with appealing foliage that will quickly soften the angularity and rawness of any new paving, include lady's mantle (*Alchemilla mollis*, opposite) and robust clump-forming *Sisyrinchium striatum* or satin flower (right).

Planting in paving

Where pavers are laid or grouted with sand, it is easy to excavate small planting slots (2.5cm/1in is ample); cement mortar needs careful chipping out with a cold chisel and club hammer. Choose a young plant and trim the rootball until it fits the slot, or sow seeds direct in a mixture of equal parts universal potting compost and grit.

Suitable plants

Dwarf thymes, pennyroyal and Corsican mint, with flowers that attract bees and mats of tiny leaves that fill the air with aromatic oils when trodden on.

Arenaria, sagina, sandworts (*Minuartia*) and mouse-ear hawkweed (*Hieracium pilosella*), with tightly massed foliage and a moss-like texture.

Various alpine cinquefoils (*Potentilla* species) revel in sunny spots, with their bright yellow flowers and leaves like those of strawberries.

The enhanced drainage and reflected warmth characteristic of hollow wall beds (left) supply a congenial habitat for succulents and sun-loving plants including sedums, sempervivums and fragrant thymes.

Sisyrinchiums and small crocuses (especially *C. tommasinianus*), which seed themselves happily and harmlessly in any cracks.

Thrift, chamomile, *Anthemis montana* and Mount Atlas daisy (*Anacyclus*), all ground-hugging plants to pack into slab-size gaps.

Mat-forming acaenas, aubrietias, campanulas, *Erinus alpinus*, *Phlox subulata* and *Trifolium repens*.

Planting hollow walls

- Dwarf shrubs and prostrate plants are ideal subjects, especially if boosted with pots of seasonal bulbs or bedding plunged to their rims in between. Permanent plants could include dwarf hebes, genistas and willows, plus aurinia and lithodora, and trailing rosemary or marjorams to cascade over the sides.
- Alternatively explore the huge range of alpines that enjoy the improved drainage, especially if you can mix some extra grit into the soil. Try plants like the various androsace, arenaria, dianthus, primula and saxifrage species and cultivars.

RAISED BEDS

Where open ground is unavailable – in a soil-less yard, say, or a mortared pavement – raised beds can offer a range of planting opportunities, and if you find bending a problem may even make gardening a positive delight.

They have other advantages too. Depending on their construction, the sides and edges can be decorated with alpines, trailers and natural wall species, while plants growing on top are nearer the eye for close appreciation. The shape, materials and alignment of their walls can echo and complement the patio layout and give enclosed spaces extra shelter. And they are versatile, offering scope for built-in seating or place settings for outdoor dining, or a raised plinth for a water centrepiece.

Beds can be designed as islands, accessible from all sides, or may be built round the boundary to reinforce the sense of enclosure and privacy. A boundary bed could be a simple hollow wall – two skins of brickwork, perhaps, flanking a gap only 15cm (6in) wide – or may be large enough to grow vegetables, plant with prostrate species like thyme or chamomile, or even turf over to make a raised lawn for seating and sunbathing.

Construction guide

Beds may be any shape provided they suit the size and style of your patio. To make sure all parts are within easy reach for maintenance, limit the maximum width to about 90cm (3ft) if working from one side only or twice that where a bed is accessible from both sides.

They can also be any comfortable height or a combination of different interlocking levels. Remember that larger and deeper beds contain more soil, and their extra weight may be a problem on roofs or decking with rudimentary foundations.

A raised bed next to a wall should be separated by a gap at least 8cm (3in) wide to permit free ventilation. Unless based directly on the soil, beds must have seep holes near their base to drain their contents, together with transverse drainage channels if the beds are built across the fall of the patio floor.

Building materials

Timber Pressure-treated boards or marine plywood are pleasant to work and handle, and easily repaired or moved if necessary. Treat any saw cuts you make during construction with preservative. Completed walls can be left natural, painted in bold or unobtrusive shades, or even clad with metal sheeting for a modern finish.

Railway sleepers Expensive, heavy to manoeuvre and difficult to cut or drill, but their weathered texture gives these salvaged units instant appeal and their bulk means that walls grow quickly.

The large dimensions of these square raised beds offer ample rooting space for their contents and match the generous scale of the adjacent steps.

Stone, bricks Sympathetic materials, especially if you source reclaimed supplies. Lay them in a bond (bridge joints with pieces in the next layer), either dry or bedded in mortar.

Concrete This can be mixed and poured *in situ* between wooden formers or shuttering (with added pigment for permanent colour), or used in the form of pre-cast slabs and blocks for building like brickwork. Soften an unwelcome brutal finish by painting with yoghurt or a manure slurry to encourage moss and algae.

PLANTING IN GRAVEL

Where it is a component of the patio floor and underlain with a weed-suppressant (geotextile) membrane, gravel can be used as a special habitat for those plants that enjoy perfect drainage around their stems. Many of these are scree plants – alpine species that grow naturally in

Plants to grow in gravel

Most alpine and rock garden subjects, especially *Alyssum montanum*, androsaces, dwarf aquilegias and phloxes, *Erinus alpinus*, edelweiss (*Leontopodium alpinum*), raoulias, sempervivums and *Silene schafta*.

loose mountain rock beds – but many other small or prostrate plants like these spartan conditions.

Introducing plants to a gravelled area

Scrape back the gravel to reveal the membrane, cut a cross in the membrane with a sharp knife and turn back the flaps. For very small plants, simply cut round a pot to remove a circle of the material.

Plant so that the top of the rootball is level with the soil surface, backfill the planting hole with topsoil mixed with

grit, replace the cut flaps under the plant's foliage and level the gravel once more.

PATIO CONTAINERS

Almost all plants can be grown in containers, which can vary in size and style from small hollowed-out stones or logs for miniature ferns, through the more familiar range of clay and plastic flowerpots, to large wooden Versailles boxes or concrete drainage pipes suitable for topiary or fruit trees. Provided it will hold compost and drain surplus

The ultimate in adaptability, containers are equally indispensable for the formal display of choice plants (above) and for tucking in here and there to reinforce permanent plants growing in the open ground (left).

One advantage of container culture is that seasonal flowers like these spring tulips can star centre stage on the patio while in bloom, after which they may be replaced in the pot with later-flowering species or simply moved to continue growing out of the spotlight.

moisture, any receptacle can be used, new or recycled, purpose-made or improvised.

You will often find that tending plants in containers allows more flexibility than keeping them in the open ground. They can be grown where there is no garden at all and, if potted in portable containers, are easily moved around the patio according to the season, to follow the sun or shelter from the cold. Displays are easily restaged to bring flowering plants into prominence and hide those past their best. Exacting plants can be given special compost mixtures – lime-free for blueberries and rhododendrons, for example, or gritty for cacti and succulents.

Container types

Clay Earthenware and terracotta pots are traditional and havc a warm, congenial appearance. Although available in a huge size range, those with diameters of 15–20cm (6–8in) upwards are the most useful for patio display. Some are easily broken if carelessly handled, and not all kinds are reliably frost-proof.

Plastic Some styles look very utilitarian, but larger sizes can be decorative, even brightly coloured. Plastic pots are often stronger and more durable than appearance might suggest, and lighter for moving around than other materials. They have good moisture retention, but some plastics become brittle after constant outdoor exposure.

Stone Heavy but impressive and very durable, and often a conspicuous feature whether planted or not. True crafted stone is much more expensive than reconstituted imitations, which can nonetheless look quite authentic. Plants grow well in either.

Wood The ideal material for making your own containers, whether square classic topiary containers or simple window boxes for sills and ledges. Half-barrels are sturdy and capacious, suitable for shrubs, trees and collections of smaller plants, or for turning into patio water gardens.

Metal Zinc and galvanized steel look traditional, aluminium and stainless steel very up-to-date. Elegant or industrial in appearance, they can echo their hard surroundings and give a contrasting hint of precision to informal plantings. Rust on mild steel can be appealing.

Basketwork Wire, cane, split bamboo and other woven materials look light and airy, adding rustic charm or contemporary simplicity to hanging or standing baskets. All kinds need a durable liner to retain soil and moisture.

Container care

Potted plants depend on you for their nutrition. Check them regularly for water – daily in hot weather – and feed every ten to fourteen days from about six weeks after planting or repotting.

In addition to drainage holes at their base, containers need a good layer of drainage material (pebbles, broken tiles, polystyrene fragments) inside before you start filling them with compost.

Strong winds can be worse than sunshine for drying foliage and compost. Move leafy plants and smaller containers into more sheltered positions, especially in winter and spring when they are more vulnerable.

Bring tender plants and thin-walled containers indoors in frosty weather or wrap them up with insulating materials: allowing a pot to freeze solid can be lethal to roots.

Repot plants into fresh compost every spring. Larger containers can be revived by replacing the top 5–8cm (2–3in) of old compost with a fresh supply.

Specimen plants for patio containers

Amelanchier lamarckii, genetically dwarf peaches and apricots, Mexican orange (*Choisya ternata*), *Prunus incisa* 'Kojo-no-mai', sacred bamboo (*Nandina domestica*), standard *Wisteria sinensis*, strawberry tree (*Arbutus unedo*), sweet bay (*Laurus nobilis*), variegated *Osmanthus heterophyllus*, *Viburnum* x *bodnantense* 'Dawn', and (in lime-free compost) *Camellia japonica*, *Magnolia stellata* and *Rhododendron yakushimanum.*

Long-lived woody subjects such as shrubs and trees (opposite) grow best in large containers where they can remain undisturbed for years, apart from annual top-dressing with fresh compost. For such long-term schemes, choose containers that are objects of beauty in their own right.

MAKING PLANTS COMFORTABLE

Patio plants are often clearly visible from the house or seating areas, so they are likely to receive more care and prompt attention when in need than their counterparts in the surrounding garden. This is just as well because they are more susceptible than open-ground plants to weather fluctuations and extremes, and you need to take special measures to keep them in good heart.

SOIL AND COMPOST

The soil in the ground is part of the wider environment and is buffered against change, whereas the contents of raised beds and the even more limited supply in containers can dry out rapidly, especially in hot sunny positions. Nutrients are in finite supply too, and must be topped up at regular intervals, particularly in soil-less compost mixes, which normally contain only soluble feeds that are soon exhausted.

Plants in exposed positions such as balconies and rooftop patios are very susceptible to drying from wind and sun, particularly if growing in metal containers, which can rapidly heat up, so regular and frequent watering is essential.

Filling beds

Start with a good balanced mixture of soil and organic matter. The topsoil removed during construction is ideal if mixed with organic materials, which hold water and release nutrients as they decay: garden compost, bagged manures, leafmould and spent hops or mushroom compost are all suitable. Soil-based potting compost is an acceptable but expensive alternative for beds, unless you can buy it in bulk. Add a recommended dressing of slow-release fertilizer and mix in thoroughly.

First spread a substantial layer of rubble in the bottom for drainage – up to one-quarter of the total depth is not excessive and can reduce the cost of soil or compost. Cover this with a layer of plastic mesh. Turf stripped from the site can be spread upside down on top before filling the bed to the rim with the planting mixture. Leave to consolidate for several weeks or tamp firm with a stake or post if you intend to plant immediately. Be prepared to top up any settlement, and add more organic material annually in late spring, either as a mulch or forked into the top 10cm (4in).

Compost for containers

Wherever possible use a compost that contains soil. As well as keeping their vitality for longer, soil-based potting composts are heavier than soil-less mixtures and give containers more stability in open positions. They also drain well – perhaps a little too fast for some woodland and bog plants, although these will be satisfied if the final 5–8cm (2–3in) of their containers is filled with a layer of soil-less compost.

Before filling containers spread a 5cm (2in) drainage layer in the bottom, and cover this with plastic mesh to stop the compost filtering down or horticultural fleece if you also want to exclude worms. Use an ericaceous (lime-free) compost for acid-loving plants such as ericas, azaleas and pieris; mix grit and compost in equal proportions for alpines and succulents, and top their containers with a 1–2cm (½–¾in) mulch of grit.

WATERING STRATEGIES

Watering is a large part of the care routine, especially for smaller containers with a limited volume of compost. To delay or reduce the need to water:

- Line porous containers (clay and wood, for example) with plastic sheeting perforated in places.
- Waterproof the inside of stone and brick walls and containers with several coats of sealant.
- Add dry granules of water-retaining gel to compost

when filling baskets and small containers (but not in autumn, to avoid soggy conditions over winter).

- Reduce evaporation by mulching the surface with loose materials like bark, gravel, grit or stones according to the style of planting.
- In a drought gather small pots together and plunge them to their rims in a large container or deep tray of shingle or used compost. Keep this moist to delay pots drying out.
- Consider installing micro-irrigation, using a system of supply pipes and individual drip lines to carry water automatically to pots from a reservoir.
- A perforated hose or trickle pipe can be used to keep whole beds moist. Lay it on the surface and cover with a thick mulch.

WINTER CARE

A few simple precautions can help plants to survive the winter months unscathed.

- Metal containers conduct low temperatures quickly, so line the inside with thick newspaper before filling with compost.
- Do not feed after early autumn, and avoid nitrogenous fertilizers after the longest day as these make plants soft.
- Delay cutting down herbaceous perennials until spring: the top growth shelters wildlife, helps insulate dormant crowns and can look spectacular embroidered with frost.

Although perhaps no longer inviting as an outdoor room, the patio in winter can still look beautiful, especially when decorated with delicate hoar frost highlights or a fresh dressing of snow.

- Keep a supply of fleece, bubble wrap or old blankets for covering containers when cold weather is forecast.
- Assemble small and thin containers in a group to make covering them easier, choosing a sheltered spot out of cold winds.

At winter's end

Celebrate the approach of spring by cleaning the patio. You can hire a pressure washer, which is easy to use and thorough, or use a stiff broom with sand and water to scour off grime and slippery films of algae. As the weather improves check furniture and containers to see if they need washing down or repainting. When plants finally show signs of growing again, you can start repotting and topdressing beds and containers, ready for the new patio season.

INDEX

Page numbers in *italics* refer to captions to the illustrations